WALKING
in
CAPTAIN COOK'S
FOOTSTEPS

by

J.Brian Beadle

First published in Great Britain in 2003 by Trailblazer Publishing (Scarborough)
www.trailblazerbooks.co.uk

ISBN 1 899004 46 7

Trailblazer
Unit 1
R/O 9 Market Place
Pickering
YO18 7AA

MAPS
The maps in this book are not to scale and are for guidance only. They do not accurately portray the right of way. It is the readers responsibility not to stray from the right of way and it is strongly advised that you take the relevant Ordnance Survey map with you on the walk.

WARNING
Whilst every effort has been made for accuracy neither the publisher nor the author bear responsibility for the alteration, closure or portrayal of rights of way in this book. It is the readers responsibility not to invade private land or stray from the public right of way for walkers. All routes in the book should be treated with respect and all precautions taken before setting out. Any person using information in this book does so at their own risk.

Cover Picture by
the Author of the
Endeavour weather
vane on the west
cliff at Whitby

CONTENTS

JUST A FEW WORDS

James Cook was born on October 27th 1728 in the tiny village of Marton. There are no remains of the cottage where the family lived. He was one of eight children of which only three survived to adulthood. His father was a farm labourer and was offered the post of Bailiff at Aireyholme Farm near Great Ayton. The village had a population of over 500 and the villagers were mainly employed in the making of cloth. It was James father's employer who noticed that James was a bright lad and paid the penny a week for him to go to school in the village. He learned arithmetic which was to help him in future years as a navigator. James left school at the age of twelve and worked for a short time on the farm. He would have climbed Roseberry Topping, the Cleveland Hills and Highcliff Nab many times. From these high vantage points he would have a good view of the sea and the sailing ships heading off to distant ports. James schooling came in useful for him when he was apprenticed to Mr Sanderson in Staithes in the Grocer/Drapers shop. But James became restless as he talked to sailors and felt a call for adventure and a life at sea. Mr Sanderson noticed this and recommended him to a shipowner in Whitby - John Walker. James stayed at the Walker house in Grape Lane, now the Cook Museum, where he studied seamanship and best of all, Navigation. He soon advanced in rank sailing colliers for Mr Walker then left to join the Navy at the age of twenty six. Within a couple of years he had his Master's certificate and five years later married Elizabeth Batts. It is about this time Cook started his voyages of discovery. In 1768 his first great voyage was on the HM Bark Endeavour which was in

THE ENDEAVOUR OFF WHITBY

Whitby in the style of the Whitby colliers he knew so well. They fitted his purpose admirably being of solid build and having facilities for a large amount of provisions, were easily sailed with a small crew and having a shallow draught allowed him to anchor close inshore. Cook's first voyage of discovery took him to New Zealand and Australia in the Endeavour. The second voyage was in the Resolution and was to try to find a Southern Continent. This voyage was special in respect to navigation. On board the Resolution Captain Cook had a chronometer, a ship's clock, it had been designed by John Harrison and for the first time allowed Cook and future navigators to accurately predict their position of longitude. The third voyage, also in the Resolution was to find a North – West passage, connecting the Atlantic to the Pacific. He was stopped by the ice so he turned south to reach Hawaii where he died at the hands of the natives on 14th February 1779. His body, or what was left of it, was reclaimed and buried at sea. Such a wonderful career came to a sudden end, he had no surviving children but his wife, now living in Surrey survived another thirty six years.

There are many memories in Cleveland of Captain James Cook which we will find as we walk the footpaths and bridleways of this beautiful land. Whether the young James Cook walked on them I do not know, but I like to think he did and that we are truly walking in Captain Cook's footsteps!

THE ENDEAVOUR

ON A CLEAR DAY

O n a clear day from the top of Roseberry Topping, which rises over 1000ft above Cleveland, you can see as far as County Durham in the north and the coast and Teesside in the east. The unusual shape of Roseberry Topping was fashioned by mining operations many years ago whilst looking for Jet and iron ore. As you leave Roseberry Topping to walk to Airy Holme Farm try to think what life might have been like in the days of James Cook. Young James only eight years old, spent some of his childhood roaming these fields and probably the Topping as well which would have given him a good view of the sea from the summit. His father was appointed Bailiff by the lord of the manor and the family moved to Airy Holme Farm. James left the farm when he was sixteen to work in a grocers shop in Staithes.

The Facts

Distance - 7½ miles/12km
Time - 3 hours
Start/Grid Ref - Gribdale Gate near Great Ayton, grid ref. 593111
Map - OS Outdoor Leisure 26
Refreshments - None on route but there are cafes and pubs in Great Ayton
Public Toilets - Great Ayton

Your Route

L eave the car park at Gribdale Gate to join a path at the Cleveland Way sign. Immediately go right onto a wide bridleway, do not climb the stone steps! It is a long but gentle climb up this wide, rough track but soon you are on the moor. At a double bend keep straight ahead ignoring the track off to the left. Ignore all other tracks to keep straight ahead still climbing gently across the moor. Eventually the track falls into a griff then climbs out again bearing right. There are good views now across the green valley on the right towards the distant hills. Soon you arrive at a junction of tracks and a gate onto a road. Go left at the bridleway sign onto another wide sandy track. Still climbing gently as you walk over the moor good views appear across to the coast and the hills around Guisborough. After a while you reach the summit and start your descent towards the forest. At the forest go through the gate turning immediately left onto a forest track. As the track climbs look for a gate on the left, pass through the gate onto the moor climbing as you go. As you approach the top of the hill the summit of Roseberry Topping rises spectacularly in front of you. The path you are on takes you towards a gate in the wall on your right. Pass through the gate then go downhill on the stone path. You now have a choice of routes. You can either ascend Roseberry Topping which I recommend, or take the easy way out and turn left through the large gate on the left at the base of the topping. If you choose the gate continue along straight ahead across the field to join a farm road at another gate/stile. If you climb Roseberry Topping take the rough exit path on the left down the rear of the Topping. It is quite arduous but soon ends at a small gate. Keep straight ahead through the gate to meet the same farm track and gate/stile as in the first option. Pass over the stile and keep on to the Cook's Airy Holme Farm passing in front of the farm to exit onto the road. At the 'T' junction turn left onto a narrow road past some houses. Keep climbing until you come to a telephone box on your left and Cockshaw Cottage on your right. Leave the road here to walk onto a private road straight ahead. Don't worry it is also a public footpath! Keep on the path over a couple of stiles and a gate as it climbs and exits into the car park at Gribdale Gate.

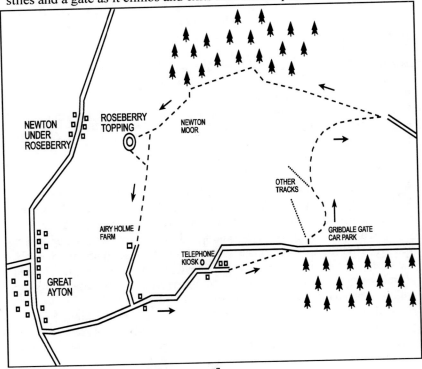

EXPLORING AROUND STAITHES

Imagine the scene at Staithes in the 18th century - no harbour wall to protect the houses that were frequently damaged by the sea, mouldy thatched roofs on the squalid little houses with queer little windows - fisherman laden down with nets and crab pots and wearing Guernsey frocks and sou'westers. The women would have bare feet and fetched water from the beck in wash tubs - with the whole place stinking of fish! Not a very good place for the young James Cook to start an apprenticeship with draper and grocer Sanderson! James must have thought that as well for as he sniffed the salt sea air into his nostrils he sensed adventure in a life at sea, no doubt encouraged by many a fishermans tale! He soon became unsettled and left Staithes to learn navigation in Whitby and start a life of adventure on the high seas. Before the outer wall of the harbour was built Staithes regularly took a battering from stormy seas, damaging property near to the shore. The Cod & Lobster pub was rebuilt more than once and Sanderson's Drapers and Grocers was smashed to pieces after James left!

The Facts

Distance - 4½ miles/7km
Time - 2½ hours
Start/Grid Ref - Staithes, grid ref. 782184
Map - OS Landranger 94 or OS Outdoor Leisure 27
Parking - At top of hill in the modern village
Refreshments - Small tea shop overlooking harbour, pubs in Staithes, pubs at Port Mulgrave & Dalehouse
Public Toilets - In car park

Your Route

Start from the car park in modern Staithes at the top of the hill leading to Old Staithes. Walk down the steep hill into the old village and marvel at the old houses and shops that haven't changed in a hundred years. Continue along through quaint old streets to the harbour where you will find the Cod & Lobster pub. Turn right here to ascend the cobbled road to the cliff top. Follow the Cleveland Way signs to the left and all the way along the cliffs to Port Mulgrave. Take to the road here and follow it around to the right through Port Mulgrave to bear left to Hinderwell. As you pass the church take a look at Hilda's Well in the graveyard. Hinderwell took its name from the well. At the main road cross almost straight across along Porret Lane following it around left for a few yards before turning right onto a public footpath where marked. This path winds its way through the houses to exit onto a muddy road at a farm. Cross the road onto a narrow track to reach another muddy road. Go straight ahead now for a few yards and when the road bends left keep straight ahead into a field over a stile where there is a sign 'please keep to path'. Cross the field to another stile then turn right down the hill over a stile with a dog gate into the wood and to a stream. Cross a footbridge over the stream then climb steeply up the other side to a field. Keep straight ahead now following a well worn path through the field into a wood. Take the path on the right on entering the wood. Keep straight ahead through the wood passing a yellow waymark then exit over a stile onto a wide grassy path. Pass a stile without a fence and continue along to a steep incline, then over a stile into a caravan site. Leave the site through a gate turning right over the bridge at the sign for Dalehouse. At the road go right up the hill past the Fox & Hounds pub to the main road. Turn right then in a few yards cross the road and turn left at the sign for 'Staithes ½ mile' to return to the car park.

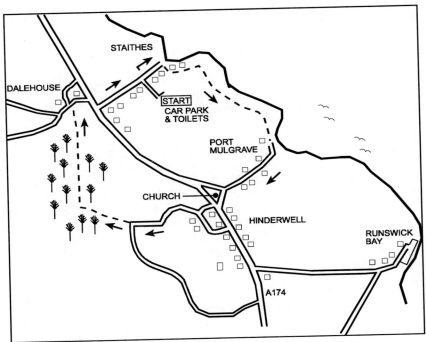

WALKING THE CLEVELAND STREET

The Cleveland Street has been in use since Roman times but was perhaps at its busiest as a medieval trade route linking the outlying regions of Cleveland and North Yorkshire to the market town of Guisborough. Maybe James Cook or his parents used it to visit the local markets or to continue along to Loftus on their way to Whitby. Early records tell us that the residents of Skinningrove were fined for not repairing their section of highway known as 'middle street'. They must have made a poor job of the repairs because all that is left now is a footpath from Guisborough to Loftus. Long before the medieval trade route it was known as Via de Witbei or Back Street. Apart from being used as a trade route it could have been used in time of war. It would have been an easy march for soldiers as well as giving them a height advantage over their enemies. The Romans had a series of signal stations on the high cliffs in this area, could it have been used by them to march their soldiers from the training camps at Cawthorne near Pickering to the coastal stations of Goldsborough and Huntcliffe? Let us walk 'The Street' and form our own conclusions as we perhaps walk where young James might have done.

The Facts

Distance - 9 miles or 20 miles if the Cleveland Way return route is used (14.4km or 32km)
Time - 3 hours (7 hours)
Start/Grid Ref - Guisborough Priory, grid ref. 618161
Map - OS Landranger 94 or OS Outdoor Leisure 26
Parking - Choice of car parks in Guisborough, follow signs
Refreshments - Pubs and snack bars in North Skelton, Carlin How and Loftus. On route at the Fox & Hounds at Slapewath
Public Toilets - In the refreshment houses

The Route

The only part left as a navigable footpath starts at Guisborough Priory and ends at Loftus. The whole route has been waymarked with either tall posts or small waymark arrows so I will not give you much in the way of route instructions. Start from the short stay car park adjacent to the church near the Priory. Leave from the rear of the car park and walk between the church and the houses. Continue along a paved way to a metal gate. Go right here onto a path which gives magnificent views to the right of the remains of the Priory. At the road go left then in a few yards turn right at the public footpath sign and waymark post at the entrance to Foxdale Farm. Several stiles

and the odd gate later you reach the road. Turn right here then in a few yards join a gravel road heading towards the trees, look on the left at the trees and

GUISBOROUGH PRIORY

you will see the waymark. You soon join the roadside footpath however and walk uphill. At the top of the hill go left to cross the road and enter a small road. Pass a post waymark hidden in the hedge then bear right past the cottages towards the Fox & Hounds Inn. At the Inn take the narrow bridleway on the left of the Fox and Hounds and climb steadily upwards passing through many gates and stiles, (all waymarked). Keep following the waymarks and climbing over stiles and you will exit onto a road.

Go left here and in about 100yds go right onto a wide road/path at the waymark post. Soon the road bends right, go straight ahead here between a pair of stone posts. If of portly build you might have to use the gate! Follow the obvious waymarked path over several stiles keeping straight ahead at all times except where the path has been re-routed, but it is obvious. Eventually you meet the road at a bridge. Turn right then almost immediately left onto a wide track which soon narrows and takes you to North Skelton, keep straight ahead to the main road running through the village. Turn right at the road then after two bridges turn right again over the cattle grid along a wide public footpath and waymark post. At the brow turn left over a stile at the yellow waymark. Keep straight ahead to another stile then to a stream and yet another stile. Cross the bridge then over the fields to two more stiles past the old Lumpsey Mine. Cross the mineral railway line then cross a disused railway track keeping straight ahead up the slope to reach a wooden stile. At the road keep straight on over the stile then across the field to another stile. Keep following waymarks eventually exiting on a narrow path to reach Carlin How. Keep straight ahead down the street, cross the road keeping almost straight ahead to the main road. Cross at the pedestrian crossing in front of you.

Cross the road and turn right then immediately left turning almost immediately right downhill along a wide track at the waymark post. In 100yds leave the wide track and keep straight ahead over the bridge. At the road turn left, cross the bridge then turn right at the sign for the Tom Leonard Mining Museum.

(If you are using the return route described below you could miss out the last part of the Street and walk past the mining museum and follow the road to the narrow metal bridge at the last cottages. See text below for rest of route.)

Go through the car park to the museum entrance. Pass under the arch at the entrance then look out for a path between the Museum and a terrace of houses straight in front of you and climb up the steps soon turning right onto a footpath. Head off following waymarks soon to join a wide track and leave the field through a gate onto the farm road. After crossing several stiles you arrive at the main road, turn right along it to the end of the Cleveland Street in Loftus.

OPTIONAL RETURN ROUTE

The Cleveland Street is a linear route so you will have to arrange transport or catch the bus for your return journey. If you would like to make a circular walk I suggest you use the Cleveland Way path which is marked on the Ordnance Survey map and well signposted so I will only give you a brief description which continues from the *italic* instructions above. Go left in front of the cottages, do not cross the bridge. Soon you must climb diagonally upwards at the Cleveland Way waymark post to take the cliff path.

There are many interesting features on the return route, look out for the metal sculptures on the high cliffs near Huntcliffe. They were commissioned to represent industry in the area. Further along you will see a plaque at the site of the Roman signal station at Huntcliffe, I will leave you to find out about the bodies in the Well!

The Cleveland Way leaves the cliff at Saltburn, which has a good Tourist Information Centre with lots of walking and historical books. The route then follows Skelton Beck for some time passing the site of Marske Mill, an ancient water mill. Towering above you is a magnificent viaduct which carries trains on the Mineral Railway taking minerals from the local mines to join the main line. After passing under the viaduct the route bears uphill and over the fields to Skelton. Past Skelton the route goes along a track known as Airy Hill Lane, look out for Cleveland Way signs, giving magnificent views across Cleveland. After a long climb and a steep descent you meet the road at Slapewath where you can have something to eat and drink at the Fox & Hounds before returning on the roadside footpath to Guisborough.

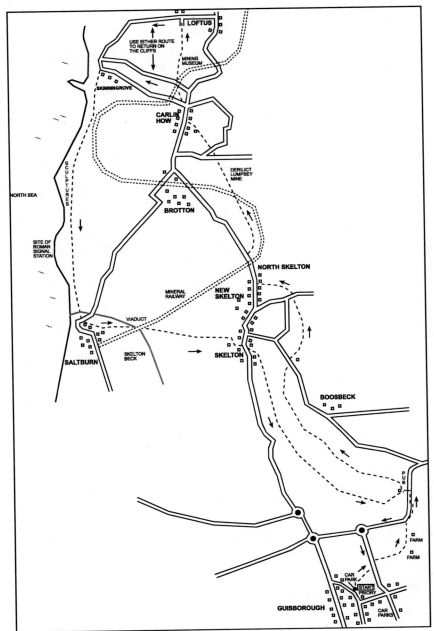

A TOUR OF COOK'S WHITBY

Whitby, famous for Whaling, Kippers, the great Abbey on the cliff, prehistoric crocodiles, dinosaurs the penny hedge and of course Captain James Cook. Let us take a walk to discover some of these treasures in this grand old town. We can climb the steps to St. Mary's Abbey or saunter along Henrietta Street to seek out an old smokehouse. But let us not forget why we are here. We are looking for evidence of James Cook and trying to walk where he might have walked as man and boy. We will pay a visit to the museum devoted to him which is in the house where he lodged as an apprentice whilst learning seafaring skills and then

THE ENDEAVOUR
WEATHER VANE

perhaps wander up the Khyber Pass to see his statue. But enough of me waffling on let's take a walk by the seaside.

The Facts

Distance - 1½ miles/2.4km
Time - 2 hours
Start/Grid Ref - Abbey car park Whitby, grid ref. 904113
Map - Outdoor Leisure 27 but better still a street map of Whitby
Parking - Abbey car park
Refreshments - Lots of choice in Whitby
Public Toilets - At the start and several on route

Your Route

Leave the Abbey car park turning right along the road. Soon go right along Green Lane and enjoy the grand views across the River Esk and the harbour. At the bottom of the hill cross the road then turn right to walk along the harbour side. Pass a car park on your left and when it ends go left along Grape Lane. Soon you will see a house on the left that belonged to John Walker, the young James Cook lived on the top floor with other apprentices when he was learning seamanship and navigation, the house is now the Cook Memorial Museum which you must visit. Leave the museum to continue along Grape Lane then turn left across the bridge. Once across go right along the side of the harbour. When you reach the pier follow the road around to the left into the Khyber Pass. Take the path to cut the corner off then cross the road and climb the steps to the top of the cliff. At the top is Captain Cook's Statue and a weather vane with his ship on top. This is a good viewpoint to watch the replica Endeavour sail into Whitby harbour. Walk straight ahead keeping the statue on your right and in about 100 yards cross the road and turn left. This road leads eventually to the shops in Skinner Street. There you will find delicious cakes and sandwiches at Bothams shop or if you prefer, a light meal in the restaurant above, both are recommended. At the end of Skinner Street turn right then left at the roundabout. On the left you pass Pannet Park and the museum which has a great Cook collection. At the bottom of the hill go left and at the roundabout left again to the Swing Bridge, you will see Endeavour Quay on the right. Cross the bridge then second left along Church Street. Follow this round right at the end then at the steps bear left along Henrietta Street to the smokehouse which is on the right. With your superb oak smoked kippers return to the steps and climb to the top. Have a look in the quaint church then follow the road past the Abbey back to the car park.

CAR PARK
START
ST. MARY'S CHURCH
ABBEY
SMOKE HOUSE
199 STEPS
DONKEY ROAD
① CAPTAIN COOK MUSEUM
NORTH SEA
CAR PARK
SWING BRIDGE
HARBOUR
HARBOUR
ENDEAVOUR WHARFE
TOURIST INFOR-MATION CENTRE
KHYBER PASS
CAPTAIN COOK'S STATUE
SPA
PANNET PARK
MUSEUM
RAILWAY STATION

A WALK IN THE CLEVELAND HILLS

I 'll take you to the fringes of Captain Cook country this time for a fabu-
lous walk in the Cleveland Hills. There are grand views all round, even
the car park has a wonderful view of Captain Cook's Monument and Roseberry Topping. I walked the route on a still day in February when there was
a dusting of snow on the hills, it was pure magic.

The Facts

Distance - 9½ miles/15km
Time - 4-5 hours
Start/Grid Ref - Clay Bank car park, grid ref. 572036
Map - OS Landranger 93&94 or OS Outdoor Leisure 26
Refreshments - The Buck Inn at Chop Gate, a little way off route
Public Toilets - At the pub

Your Route

There is a good car park at the top of Clay Bank but it soon becomes full.
Alternative parking is on the wide grass verge. Leave along the road
towards Bilsdale in a southerly direction. In a couple of hundred yards turn
left through a gate following a sign for the Cleveland Way. It is quite a
climb along this well-defined footpath with a short scramble onto the moor,
although there is an alternative route on the left. Once onto the moor keep to
the wide path straight ahead. In about two miles turn right along a wide
track. Then in about a mile where the wide track goes left take the bridleway
straight ahead through the heather and down the hill. In a few yards keep
straight ahead down the steep track and through a gate or stile in the stone
wall. The path meanders along to the hamlet of Town Green then on to the
village of Seave Green, passing through two farm gates. At the road turn left
down the hill, over the bridge across Bilsdale Beck and onto the main road.
Left here along the roadside footpath for a few hundred yards to Chop Gate.
(*If you wish to visit the Buck Inn keep straight on into the village.*) Turn
right opposite the war memorial onto the Carlton road then immediately
right again past the Chapel along the public bridleway. A long uphill trek
now leads onto Cold Moor. This overgrown path varies from woodland
glade, country lane to open moor. Keep straight ahead at all times finally
reaching the moor through a farm gate. Follow the worn track in a northerly
direction that leads over the top of Cold Moor, eventually reaching the es-
carpment edge at Broughton Bank, turn right at the junction to follow the
Cleveland Way again down a steep hill. Pass through the gate at the bottom

and go straight ahead towards the impressive Wainstones at the top of the opposite hill, they will be silhouetted against the sky.

The Wainstones are a magnificent outcrop of rocks that seem to be balanced precariously on the edge of the moor. There are challenging rock faces for climbers with the Sphinx Rock standing proud on the Bilsdale face. Legend says that a Danish chieftain was murdered here giving the name of the rocks Saxon origin. There is a choice of routes now, you can either take the short but exhilarating scramble through the heart of the stones or succumb to old age and take the path round to the left. At the summit stop to admire the view North to Teesside, Durham and Newcastle in the distance. Or West across to the hills of the Yorkshire Dales. Cross Hasty Bank top then in one mile turn sharp left through the rocks and down a steep hill to a stile on the left. Cross the stile and follow the Cleveland way sign down a narrow path to the road. Turn left to return to the Clay Bank car park..

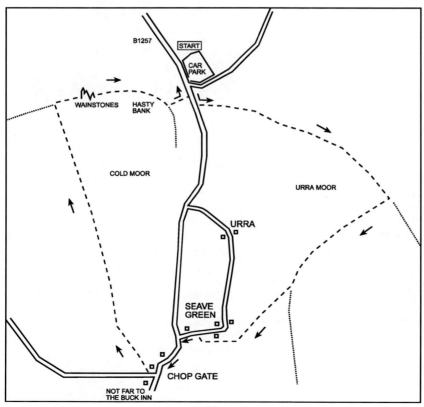

THE GREAT MONUMENT

The people of North Yorkshire and Cleveland are proud of their seafaring history so let us walk onto the Cleveland hills to visit a monument to Captain James Cook. In memory of his great achievements a Whitby banker erected a sixty foot obelisk in 1827 on the edge of the Cleveland Hills with grand views to the Pennines, Durham and the Tees. I suggest you start from Great Ayton Station, I took the train from Whitby along the Esk Valley line and enjoyed the scenic ride to Great Ayton. There are only a few trains each day and it is best to avoid the 'school run' ones if you can! If you want to take your car you could park at the station but you are

CAPTAIN COOK'S MONUMENT

missing a treat by not using the train. If you would rather start in Great Ayton and walk along the road to the station it is just down the road.

This is only a short walk but I think you will take time to climb through the forest to the monument and once you are there will not be able to rush away from the grand views all around. The climb through the forest is quite strenuous climbing almost vertically to the monument before heading downhill towards Roseberry Topping and Gribdale Gate then back to the railway station. If you would like a longer excursion you could join on to route two and ascend the topping.

The Facts

Distance - 3½ miles/5.6km
Time - A couple of hours depending on your level of fitness and how long you enjoy the view
Start/Grid Ref - Great Ayton Railway Station, grid ref. 574108
Map - OS Landranger 93 or OS Outdoor Leisure 26
Refreshments - Nothing on route but Great Ayton is only 1 mile (1.6km) away
Public Toilets - Great Ayton

Your Route

Leave the railway station then turn right over the bridge. Walk for a few hundred yards (metres) then turn right at the crossroad by the two white houses. Continue along the road until it becomes a track and starts to climb passing through a gate. Still climbing the track becomes open pasture. Keep climbing then follow the wall round to the left towards a gate into the forest. Through the gate bear right following the yellow mark on the tree. Climb up until you meet a track. Cross straight across here and continue to climb. Yes, it is steep! It is a hard, long climb to the top but well worth it if you survive! At the top bear right through the heather to Captain Cook's Monument. Remember where you came in because you must leave by turning left through a path through the heather which soon opens out into a wide, well maintained path for the Cleveland Way. Do not take the path through the stone wall! At the bottom of the hill exit by a gate then go left onto the road. At the entrance to the park take the footpath on the left downhill then at the road go straight ahead. *(If you prefer you could simply ignore the footpath and walk down the road keeping a wary eye out for traffic).* The road takes you eventually to a 'T' junction. Turn right here and in a few hundred yards you are back at Great Ayton Station.

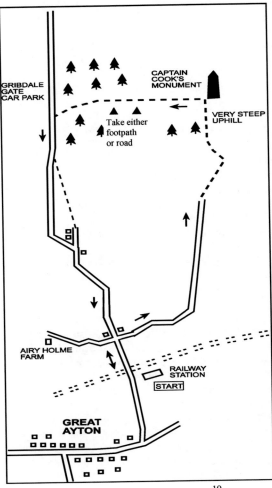

GUISBOROUGH TO HIGHCLIFF NAB

When the young James Cook lived at the family home of Airey Holme Farm he must have visited Guisborough many times. I like to think that instead of taking the road to town he would have taken this walk to High Cliff Nab. He probably brought a bite to eat with him and sat on the nab enjoying the grand view across to the sea where he would have been able to watch the sailing ships. He must have felt intense excitement as he watched their huge white sails filling with a westerly wind as they headed out to sea.

The walk from Guisborough is quite a tough climb through the forest that hides the grand view almost until the last, but it is worth it as High Cliff Nab is second only to the ascent of Roseberry Topping in this area.

Whilst you are in Guisborough you might like to visit the ruins of the 12th century Priory. Follow the road into the market place (main street) and turn right, it is just around the corner.

The Facts

Distance - 6 miles (9½ km)
Time - 3 hours
Maps - OS Outdoor Leisure 26
Start- Guisborough, grid ref. 615158
Terrain- Easy forest roads
Parking– Enter Guisborough from the Whitby road, go straight ahead at the first traffic lights. The Car Park is on the right. First is a short stay and second a longer stay but usually full.
Refreshment - Excellent bacon sandwiches at kiosk in the car park
Public toilets - At start in car park

Your Route

Leave the car park and walk towards the traffic lights. Go straight ahead here towards Whitby and in a few hundred yards turn right along Butt Lane. When the road goes right go straight ahead onto a wide, rough track. At a junction of tracks bear left then continue straight ahead to the forest. Keep on the forest road as it bends to the right making its way uphill then when you meet a wide forest road go left as waymarked. At the top of the hill turn right onto a wide grassy uphill track. The track soon rejoins a forest road, go straight ahead here downhill. Shortly you arrive at a clearing and a junction of tracks. Keep straight ahead here in the direction of the waymark. A gentle climb through the forest leads to another forest road, go acute right here at the waymark for a long, hard climb. Good views appear through the trees as you reach the top. At the end of the road bear right to now follow signs for the Cleveland Way. Straight on at the next junction to soon go downhill and turn left onto another track soon passing Cleveland Way confirmation signs. Keep following the Cleveland Way signs until the forest road turns left. Go right now over a stile onto a narrow, grassy path. Soon you will see your goal as you reach a clearing at Highcliff Nab. You will linger here a while I think to enjoy the superb views over Guisborough to the coast. I wonder if the young James Cook stood on this very spot looking out to sea dreaming of a life at sea.

When you can tear yourself away from this grand place rejoin the path to follow a paved path downhill, still following Cleveland Way signs to a wide road and a signpost for the Tees Link. This points your way back to Guisborough so turn right here to go downhill on a wide, stony track. At the 'T' junction go right onto another forest road. Follow this forest road for some way as it falls and rises then at the second junction go left to return to Guisborough.

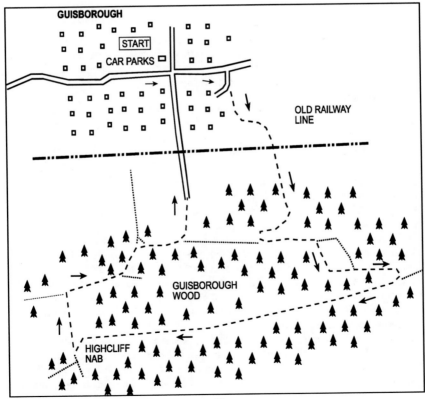

GREAT AYTON

James Cook was born at Marton and when he was eight years old the family moved to Airey Holme Farm. This had one big advantage for James as there was a school nearby in Great Ayton. Schooling had to be paid for in those days and James's father's employer, thinking he was a bright lad became his benefactor. James learned arithmetic there which was a stepping stone to becoming a navigator. James left the village when he was sixteen but his family built a house there and his Mother is buried in the graveyard at All Saints Church. The house they built was dismantled and shipped to Australia.

The Facts

Distance - 4 miles/6½ km
Time - 2 hours
Maps - OS Outdoor Leisure 26
Start - Great Ayton, grid ref. 556107
Terrain - Easy field and farm tracks
Parking - Street parking alongside stream near All Saints Church
Refreshment - Good pies from Lowther's Butchers shop on   route.
A choice of Tea Rooms in Great Ayton
Public toilets - Behind the schoolroom museum

Your Route

Start from the suggested roadside park and head off towards the town. On the left you will see a sign for All Saints Church where the Cook family would have visited. James's parents are buried there. At the junction cross the road to go straight ahead into the town, passing the pie shop on the way and shortly after the schoolroom where James was educated. Continue past the statue of James and the Royal Oak keeping on the main road. After the road bears left look out in about a hundred yards for a footpath sign and a metal kissing gate on the opposite side of the road. Cross the road and walk along the footpath through the trees. Keep straight on through several gates, a field and a copse to soon cross the Esk Valley railway line, take care!
Soon you reach a farm road, cross the road to a stile into a field. Straight ahead now still on an obvious track and start to climb towards a wood. Cross a stile into the wood then climb some stone steps to a wide path. Go right now to walk through a tunnel of trees. Soon you exit the wood into a field over a stile. Keep straight ahead to cross the field and exit onto a small road by crossing yet another stile and down a rough track. Go right now and walk as far as the crossroads. Take the road opposite past the White House and shortly after a dip in the road turn right along a farm track signed as Brookside Farm. Soon pass through a gate and over the railway bridge to arrive at Brookside Farm. Continue to the house and buildings keeping to the right of

them to exit onto a small road. At the 'T' junction go right to the area called Little Ayton. Just past the first house on the left turn left along a public footpath which leads to a footbridge. Cross the bridge into a field bearing diagonally right to the opposite corner to continue across the next field on a more distinct path to a stile in the corner of the field. Keep on the path then follow the hedge around to the right to cross a sports field. Keep straight ahead to eventually arrive at a gate and bridge over the stream and into Great Ayton. Go left now along the main street to the main road. Your car should be parked along the street opposite but if you would like to see the site of James Cook's parents house go left over the bridge. Keep straight ahead when the road goes right and soon you come to a fenced off area with a small obelisk. This is where the house was before it was shipped piece by piece to Melbourne, Australia. In return the obelisk was built with granite quarried in Victoria then shipped across to England and on to Great Ayton.

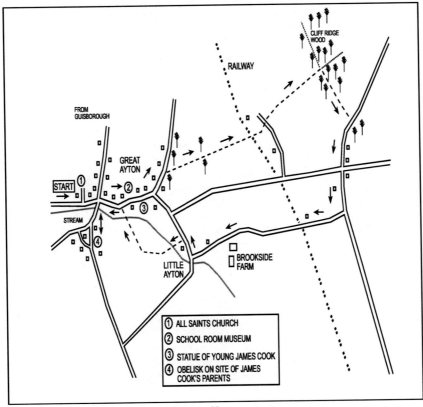

① ALL SAINTS CHURCH
② SCHOOL ROOM MUSEUM
③ STATUE OF YOUNG JAMES COOK
④ OBELISK ON SITE OF JAMES COOK'S PARENTS

OTHER TRAILBLAZER BOOKS
CYCLING BOOKS
Mountain Biking around the Yorkshire Dales
Mountain Biking the Easy Way
Mountain Biking in North Yorkshire
Mountain Biking on the Yorkshire Wolds
Mountain Biking for Pleasure
Mountain Biking in the Lake District
Mountain Biking around Ryedale, Wydale & the North York Moors
Exploring Ryedale, Moor & Wold by Bicycle
Beadle's Bash - 100 mile challenge route for Mountain Bikers

WALKING BOOKS
Walking into History on the Dinosaur Coast
Walking around the Howardian Hills
Walking in Heartbeat Country
Walking the Riggs & Ridges of the North York Moors
Short Walks around the Yorkshire Coast
Walking on the Yorkshire Coast
Walking to Abbeys, Castles & Churches
Walking around the North York Moors
Walking around Scarborough, Whitby & Filey
Walking to Crosses on the North York Moors
Walks from the Harbour
Walking in Dalby, the Great Yorkshire Forest
Ten Scenic Walks around Rosedale, Farndale & Hutton le Hole
Twelve Scenic Walks from the North Yorkshire Moors Railway
Twelve Scenic Walks around the Yorkshire Dales
Twelve Scenic Walks around Ryedale, Pickering & Helmsley

YORKSHIRE BOOKS
Curious Goings on in Yorkshire
The Crucial Guide to Crosses & Stones on the North York Moors

For more information please visit our web site:
www.trailblazerbooks.co.uk